HEART AND SOUL
REFLECTIONS:
Poems, Anecdotes and Thoughts

LORNA A. HENNINGHAM

authorHOUSE®

AuthorHouse™
1663 Liberty Drive
Bloomington, IN 47403
www.authorhouse.com
Phone: 1-800-839-8640

Published by AuthorHouse 6/7/2013

ISBN: 978-1-4817-3903-0 (sc)
ISBN: 978-1-4817-3902-3 (e)

Library of Congress Control Number: 2013906443

Any people depicted in stock imagery provided by Thinkstock are models, and such images are being used for illustrative purposes only. Certain stock imagery © Thinkstock.

This book is printed on acid-free paper.

Dedication

This book is dedicated to the following persons:
My father Egbert Williams, whom I love dearly.
My late mother Pearline Williams and grandparents James and Leah
Neufville, whose memory I will always cherish.
Miss Polly Neufville, loving and caring aunt.
My dear husband Delroy, for his long lasting love and commitment.
Last but not least, my two precious children, Orane and Jodi-Ann.

Contents

Love, Life's Lessons and Appreciation

Foreword

In this age of growing complexity, characterized by tediousness and the fleeting of time, it is a challenge to truly appreciate the generous provisions of The Gracious God. This demands moments of solitude and quietness of spirit, as the human reflects on the Divine. This experience the author chose to pursue and the result is this book of poetry.

This book of poems, anecdotes, and thoughts, is filled with inspiring words, many practical suggestions, and faith molding testimonies that will significantly strengthen and motivate Christian faith and belief in both young and mature believers. It reflects the longings of a heart of unbridled spiritual passion, conducted in a spirit of gratitude to the infinite God.

I have read these poems and to say the least, they have stimulated my thinking and inspired my belief. The reading of this book is a spiritual adventure worth pursuing. By the time you get through reading these poems, you too will be inspired and convinced about this God who Lorna Henningham writes about. I commend this work as fruitful for both Christian believers and poetry enthusiasts who are appreciative of the artistry of reflections from the human soul.

Bishop Fedlyn A. Beason, J.P., Ph.D.

Preface

Heart and Soul Reflections: Poems, Anecdotes and Thoughts, has been in the making for some time. I have finally mustered the courage to complete it. This collection of thoughts and poems is a tribute to God for His goodness and mercy, and appreciation for persons and circumstances that have shaped and molded my life. As you read, you will experience moments of inspiration, adoration, introspection and thankfullness. Despite life's frustrations, embrace the things that bring peace and happiness. My encouragement to all readers is to keep dreams, hope and talents alive through God. If you ever feel trapped or discouraged, remember that Jesus is constantly making intercession for us, and is only a prayer away. Be blessed as I share these precious and intimate experiences with you.

Acknowledgements

Foremost acknowledgement to The Triune God without whom I could not have completed this project.

My sincere gratitude to the following persons: Bishop Dr. Fedlyn A. Beason, advice and editing; Reverend Christopher J. Newton, editing and proofreading; Reverend Oral Beason, Esq., legal advice; Delroy, my husband, for ideas and support; Orane and Jodi-Ann, my children, for active participation; Bernard Neufville, uncle, for his motivation; Leonie, my sister, for typing and critique, and members of the Davie Community Worship Center who supported me in this project.

ANECDOTES AND THOUGHT TEASERS

Anecdotes

Appreciation: Appreciation rides in the same car as work well
done; be a passenger in it and join in the celebration.

Charity: Charity begins in the heart, extends from
the hands and impacts the receiver.

Dignity: Dignity worn gracefully adorns the
wearer and motivates the observer.

Failure: Failure at a task does not set the premise
for future assignments to be life sentences.

Integrity: Integrity lies within the ambit of our horizon;
it has no class, gender or color discrimination.

Nature: Nature is real beauty without the additives.

Trust: Trust is being ourselves and allowing
others to make their own judgment.

Virtue: Virtue is the apex of purity to which we all can aspire.

Words: Words spoken irresponsibly may crush someone's
ego for life and still not earn the user a distinction.

Blessed and Loaded

Accepting failure is not an option,
It is a spirit of defeat;
A non-progressive ideology.
The reverse opens our minds to the vastness
Of God's wonder and power.
Walk in favor;
Pursue goals with optimism;
Seize the handshake of opportunity as it comes;
And embrace its contents with enthusiasm.

Align purpose and passion with destiny;
Work hard with precision and integrity;
Plan wisely;
Utilize good judgment and empathy;
Don't apply brakes to empowerment;
Accept your blessings with thanksgiving;
And maximize the unique vision God invested in you.

Challenges

Challenges will come.
When they do,
Don't be afraid of intimidation.
With unwavering faith and tactile wisdom,
Hit the target where it's most vulnerable.

If we never had challenges,
How would we appreciate the feelings
Associated with winning?
When you see challenges don't run;
Step with the conviction of a winner;
Be positive about the outcome and prepare
For the next marathon.

Motivation

Confidently occupy your space;
You have a right to purposeful living.
Don't allow character assailants to derail your quest
For success, or negativity to be a deterrent.
Never subject yourself to limitations;
Negotiate life skillfully with a sense of caution;
Swim but do not succumb to contrary currents;
Surmount obstacles with a drive to survive;
Walk with uncompromised conviction;
Run with courage, stamina, and determination;
Use life's challenges to maintain altitudes of greatness;
Let it synchronize with your spirituality;
Live your life as God would have it;
Motivated, spiritually fulfilling, and full of options.

Peacemaker

Strive to be a mediator and peace facilitator
At all times;
Never light the match that ignites division;
Douse and smother the flames of confusion.
Malice is wasting valuable energy
That can be used otherwise to do good deeds;
Don't be a participant.
Hate is a conduit to the devil's territory;
A wide road leading to destruction;
Walk far from it.
Jealousy forms the basis for corrupted inclinations
To be at their worst;
Shun it.
Never go to bed angry;
Let peacemaking be a lifestyle commitment;
Soar to altitudes of greatness
And embrace God's peace initiative for your life.

Self-pity

Self-pity needs no affiliate to be destructive;
It can wreck the psyche all by itself.
When the party is over,
Piqued emotions will keep on riding;
Unless brought to a halt.
Life goes on regardless of our personal feelings.
A strong desire to survive;
And a deep resolve to be over comers
are bold initiatives.
But having God as our Father,
The Holy Spirit as our Comforter,
And Jesus Christ as our Deliverer,
Is enough motivation to mend broken pieces.

Sensitivity

If you don't enjoy the effects of pain,
Don't inflict it on others.
If you don't like being talked about negatively,
Don't initiate that conversation.
Hurtful words and actions are like sharpened knives without
handles, they can cut both user and potential victims.
A prudent person upholds wisdom, exercises
understanding and avoids insensitivity.
Think before you speak and act;
Or you might become your own victim.

THANKSGIVING

Awesome God

When I think of the intricacies of creation;
The Majestic Trio of The Godhead;
Father, Son and Holy Spirit;
I can only say, "God, You are Awesome!"

When I think of Your gift to humanity
And my encounter with Divinity
Through Jesus, Your Son,
The question is,
How could You give of Your One and Only?
Clearly, the answer is the redemption of man.

Lord, Your love is pure, measureless, reachable,
Without prejudice, limit or divide.
Lord, who can stand without awe in Your presence?
How could I take a breath of fresh air without gratitude
To The Creator of all good things?

Reverently, I stand in acknowledgement
Of Your Lordship and Supremacy.
God, I exalt You above everything.
Praises, honor and glory are Yours;
Everything belongs to You.
You allow us to be recipients of Your mercy and grace.
Thank You for the privilege, Lord.
Amen.

Connected

Personal, precious, ecstatic, pure;
Away from detractors, through my closet door;
Serene, solemn, reverent mood;
Anticipation heightens, conscience halts
And introspection begins.

His unforgettable presence fills the room;
There's savoring sweetness.
Deep within, my belly groans;
Emitting a crescendo of hallelujah and praise.

Feelings rise;
Infallible and new.
Transcending earthly realities,
Logistics and humanistic views.
Unable to keep silent,
Praise and worship ascends.
Self is slain.

Words do not adequately express the feelings
When The Holy Spirit is present.
There's closeness, depth, love incomprehensible;
Elevation to another dimension, another realm.
Spirituality supersedes self.
Every vital organ harmonizes with the vibration
Of precious moments – Really special with God.

Lord, You Are

I see and I ponder;
I hear and I wonder;
I feel and I encounter;
Lord, You are Omnipotent and Omnipresent.
To exist is to be on Your radar;
Whether up high or in the bowels of the earth;
Even throughout the universe and beyond.

In every sphere and corner, even in awkward moments;
You show dominion, there's no escape from Your presence.
In lusty raindrops and beautiful sunshine;
In caressing wind swirls, midst breathtaking flowers;
You are ever-present as Creator.

In secrecy and dark moments You illuminate paths;
In lonely hours You give comfort;
And in weakness, strength for yet another task.
In tears and sorrows, You are our Joy;
In pain, You are the Analgesic,
And in problems, You are the Solution.

You hear words unspoken and thoughts not yet materialized;
You tune into faint whispers, loud atonements, and relentless cries;
You calm tempestuous anger and still raging emotions;
You are Alpha and Omega; the past, present, and future.
I see and I ponder;
I hear and I wonder;
I feel and I encounter;
You are indeed Jehovah.

New Thing

God created a new thing in me;
It began quite instantaneously.
I can't explain, but can surely say;
Thank You, Lord, for using me this way.

I started writing one day;
Feeling inspired,
Thoughts and ideas kept coming my way.
Lord, I said, this must be Your will.
Teach me to listen, teach me to be still;
As You engage my thoughts and will.

Before this experience, I had often prayed;
Lord, let Your will on me be laid.
Let there be something wonderful to do;
As I glorify and honor You.
This inspiration I know is true;
It could only have come from You.

Lord, to You I dedicate these poems.
Bless and anoint the words I use;
Let them bring You honest dues.
Let poetry be a powerful vehicle, Lord, I pray;
To bless some household everyday.
Thank You, Lord,
For using me in this special way.

NATURE WALK

Covenant

Dear Lord, how marvelous and majestic You are
To man's existence on planet earth!
The awesomeness of Your presence is evident;
As azure tinctured lily white cotton balls
Go fleeting across the cerulean skies;
Giving rise to picturesque formations way up high.
Behold!
You are universally clear.

A rainbow appears like magic silhouetting the sky;
The sun throws a backdrop of misty colors blending into
Magnificence;
Your covenant once made is still relevant and binding;
Bringing to remembrance the unflinching promise
You gave to man.

Intrigue

Delicate fingers against receptive skin;
Leaves sensory receptors tickled, that's the wind.
The sun shines brilliantly to light the world;
Never ceasing until whisked away by the
Darkening shades of twilight.

Provocatively, the moon smiles with an occasional wink;
Nature lovers ponder at what she thinks.
Stars twinkle nightly, their constellations bright;
For moonlight lovers, that's sheer delight.

The earth in its bounteous vastness unfolds;
God's artistry at work; a sight to behold.
Green massive trees protect the watersheds;
Habitat for birds to nestle their feathered heads.

Waterfalls cascade over jagged rocks;
Carved beautifully by nature's hands.
The allure of the sea as she beckons and calls;
No prejudice or discrimination, a warm welcome to all.

God speaks in volumes powerful and strong;
Take time to enjoy the lyrics of life's songs.
Intrigue, mystical beauty, all fashioned to heal;
Nature's orchestra lies within the Master's appeal.

Night Shade

Sunlight no longer permeates the sky;
Grey mist approaches, dusk draws nigh.
Night comes quickly, birds perch on branches worn thin;
They do not sway, for there's no wind.

Crickets chirp, toads croak loudly;
Speaking in tones humans do not understand.
Indistinguishable noises blend;
Echoing ritualistic night calls.

The sea looks harmless.
The ebb and flow of its tide sounds like music to the ears;
As waves glide over rocks;
In an endless race to steal sand from the sea shore.

Brackish water carried by a sudden gust of wind;
Sprays salty moisture on faces exposed.
A fish goes shimmering, under the moonlight;
Another flicks itself above the water's surface;
Not a single fishing bird beholds that sight.

Jasmine and violet's fragrance proliferate the air;
The elusive moon elicits romantic feelings;
Eerie silence gives way to tranquility;
And deep reflective thoughts…sometimes surreal.
Tired from a hard day's work, sleep is eminent;
Then dreams take over.
With a flick of the eyes, a world of superb fantasy
Transforms into reality, but it is only a dream.

Before long, darkness evaporates, reality awakens;
The stillness of the night slips away unhindered;
Giving rise to the bustle of traffic, and the riotous noise
Of pots and pans creating a din to awaken the dawn.

Peacock's Pleasure

Proud Mr. Peacock has taken a bath;
Now he is strutting the rose garden path.
With head erect and perfect steps;
He flaunts in grandeur and acts his best.
He fluffs his tail feathers and throws a look;
To see who admires and who has been hooked.

Out comes the bellow, loud and profound;
I'm sure it was heard through the valley around.
Onlookers are mesmerized, cameras go click;
Proud Mr. Peacock employs some tricks.
Children are awed and reach out to touch;
But he does not indulge, that's asking too much.
His beads are a wonder, but teasers beware;
Don't venture too near to his attractive fan-tail.

His colors a blend of green, yellow, and blue;
With glistening feathers of shimmering hues.
Midst stunning wing-feathers there lies his appeal;
Kids know this unpretentious peacock is real.

This rare spectacle can teach us a lesson or two;
If we ourselves are only willing to be true.
God wants us, like him to be glad;
To show off our talents for His glory.

Should mean folks say we're not attractive enough;
Remember the allure of the peacock's strut.
He showed off his beauty, like him we can be;
As proud as the master designed you and me.

Silhouettes

Amidst shades of darkness, sparkling raindrops caress veins
Of silvery green,
Leaves that otherwise would not be seen.
Between broken blinds;
Beads of sunlight seep through tired droopy eyes,
Casting eerie shadows on overhanging beams.
A ribboned rainbow's portrait penetrates the daunting dusky sky;
Bringing thoughts of silhouette to the mind.

An eagle soars above intimidating clouds,
Leaving her shadows far behind;
A tulip turns her cup into beauty then fades into the earth
Which readily recaptures her waning strength.
Day kisses dusk and says goodnight;
But not before the riveting sunset ignites a kaleidoscope of colors,
From the water's edge and the looming skyline.

A little girl stands behind her mother's hips;
Pulls her apron strings;
Then peeks at the world with eyes of intrigue and nervous fright.
A dog barks and chases a cat into a maze of tangled ferns;
Depicting what cats and dogs sometimes do;
They fuss and fight.
Hope that cat makes it out alright.

Two lovers engage their hearts on history's page;
Their names are carved on barks of trees;
On which they make a pledge for life.
Their memoirs engraved in lover's accents;
Ah! The mystery of the mind and its ravishing emotions;
The complexities of life and the pleasures that evoke;
… Silhouettes …
Of life.

Transformed

Dapper, debonair, lightweight and free;
Gracefully meandering from tree to tree.
Sucking nectar, swaying in the breeze;
Sprayed with droplets, sprinkled with rain;
Sometimes daunted but not outdone;
She flaunts her beauty and has lots of fun.

From an egg to a caterpillar, a cocoon to a butterfly;
Doesn't nature testify about our Creator most high?
Why not cry, "Abba Father, you are worthy, be glorified!"
How beautiful is nature if we can't appreciate the magnificence
Of butterflies?

Like them, our lives too were transformed;
Theirs through metamorphosis, ours through redemption.
Once we were sin-stained, blindfolded and hell bent;
But God had a plan for our transformation.

He sent His Son, our lifeline to eternity;
His blood became the ransom, His life a testimony.
Jesus conquered death and hell, as He exposed His heart;
Only a love so pure could deflect the devil's dart;
But we had to do our part;
By inviting Jesus into our hearts.

Look at us!
From ashes to beauty, God's image must win.
From darkness, now a bright light shines within;
Obliterating the past.

Keep looking and listen!
From sin to grace our sins were expunged
To give us a fresh start.
Look, listen, and live!
From death to life: new vision, new hope, new appeal,
New identity;
Adoption into God's family.

Should we be fervent in prayer?
There's no other way.
Once we're consumed with God's word,
There's power to deny the flesh.
His grace is sufficient in all aspects.

Christians, we must be on the watch.
No time for snacking in the midst of combat.
Let's move forward, no more eggs or pupas but full blown,
Awe inspiring, soul saving butterflies for God.

PRAYER, FAITH AND MOTIVATION

Call Jesus

When sin looks enticing and temptation feels like fun;
When the conscience warns of danger
And the mind is all perplexed;
The devil is targeting the physical;
Wants to destroy the emotional;
And is envious of the spiritual.

Eyes perceive and images are conceived;
Soon there's desire and germination of the seed.
Don't wait for proof of the enemy's strategy;
Stop the speculation and run.

Smoke is the forerunner of a fire;
Glare suggests a problem looms;
Don't hesitate to activate the wisdom button.
With the siren from prayer and Holy Spirit direction;
Deploy and charge full force with the power.

Closer Walk

Oh for a closer walk, Dear Father;
To be near You is my prayer.
Who gives me strength and solace?
None but You, Dear Lord, I'd say;
Tomorrow I know is never promised;
But if awake, please let me say;
"Thank you, Lord, for yet another day."

Pour on me Your Anointing;
Grant, I pray, a heart like Thine.
May I mirror Your reflection;
Trod in Your footprints all the time?

Thank you for consistent comfort,
Love and favor, Lord Divine.
Love me, Heavenly Father, love me;
Grant me peace and joy sublime.

Defined by You

My Lord and visionary, define my path;
Afford me the knowledge to do my part.
Teach me to walk with You in mind;
For only in Your footsteps I am defined.

Grant patience;
Endurance is my plea;
Unravel the mysteries so complex to me.
Arduous sometimes my tasks may be;
Help me to accomplish them with integrity.

The gift of love all lives do touch;
May material things not matter too much.
Select my words and guard my tongue;
Let me glorify You in thoughts and actions.

Lord, I'm defined by You;
I'll never let go.
In my walk, talk, heart and mind;
Help me true stewardship to find.

Dream Buster

Dare you to dream, don't stop at that;
Assign them to purpose with your goals on top.
When ideas are conceived, pursue them with aggression;
Don't allow them to be blocked by circumstances
And "dream busters" who want you to stop.

The ability to dream big was implanted by our Father;
He fashioned us in His image with the potentials we've got.
His resources are unlimited;
They cannot be fathomed by the human mind;
Go, birth your dreams and see what you find.

When God grants His favor, don't ever be shocked;
"Dream stealers" will take what you've got.
Sometimes after your enemies seem to tear you piece by piece;
Suddenly there's a shift, and lo, God's grace lifts you to your feet.

You might feel invisible or trod upon;
Don't let go of God's unchanging hands.
When you are mocked, deemed crazy, and people laugh in your face;
Avail yourself of God's mercy and His unending grace.

The process might seem long;
Don't lose hope when you taste of life's challenging cup.
You've come too far to be sidetracked;
There's a bright light at the end of the tunnel.

Night is over, day breaks its fast;
Out of your belly healing waters will flow
Into streams of blessing that the world should know

God is bigger than any opposition you may face.
It does not matter your condition;
When He says yes, dreams will come true.
Dare to be a dreamer, a trendsetter, a world changer;
Dare to dream on!

Empowered

Empowered to be original;
To uphold things that are right.
Empowered to make wise choices;
To achieve God's best for our lives.

Empowered to think "out of the box"
To know when blessings are unleashed.
Empowered to push sin from our doorsteps;
And walk with authority and grace.

Empowered despite misgivings;
To replace defeat with victory.
Empowered to live undaunted;
By attacks of adversity and fright.
Empowered to move past fault-finding and
Head towards goals that define the strong;
Empowered by salvation to live as children of God.

Fear

Fear of water, fear of heights;
Fear that nothing in our lives will ever turn out right.
Fear of insects, fear of the dark;
Fear of walking in the park.
Fear of fire, fear of space;
Fear of disappearing without a trace.
Fear of the future and what it holds;
Fear of the present and what we're told.

Fear can wrap itself around anxiety, worry,
Frustration and stress;
It can be the gateway for other psychological issues
To be at their best.
Our sense of security will then become warped;
Sending rational interpretation for a walk.
Friendships and companionship it can undermine;
Who wants to partner with someone who is fearful all the time?

Fear entertained is faith denied;
It provides vacant places for the devil to hide.
He will steal, control and devour.
If we allow him, when he's finished we'll have no power.

The beliefs fear evoke once it sets in;
Can leave us with no real desire to win.
It can cause us to abort dreams and important plans;
Our destiny the devil will then hold in the palm of his hand;
Diminishing our ability to receive what God has planned.

Jesus defied gravity when He walked
On top of the water which caused much talk.
Peter boldly stepped out for this was his trait;
Fear got a hold of his mind and used it as bait.
He took his eyes off Jesus and started to think;
You know the rest of the story, he began to sink.

To conquer this fear we must believe God's words;
And speak positive messages until heard.
The devil's evidence is not true;
Put faith into action and watch it bear fruit.

Whenever you feel fearful,
Don't run to the phone just head to the throne.
God gives each person the ability to access Him on their own.
Fear is only an intruder occupying the space
Where faith should be functional in full force;
Under God's protection and His grace;
Fear not!

# Forgiveness

Holding on to resentment can lead to sin;
Unforgiveness will strengthen its roots
And bear hatred fruits.
Bitterness will rise and bondage set in;
Making you a slave to unforgiveness;
It can win.

Don't stay unapologetic
And feed malice to hate;
Stop the enemy's tactics without delay.
Forgive the person who speaks negatively and accuses you
Wrongly;
The one who hates you without a cause.

You may think it's not your fault;
You may ask,
"Do I have to be the one to forgive?"
Forgiveness is a must;
Do it for your healing and soul satisfaction;
Pave the way for The Holy Spirit's accommodation.

You can't be a loser by forgiving someone;
Once you do, God's peace grows brighter and
The weight of unforgiveness gets lighter.
Utilize your right;
Take your power back;
Give the gift of love and forgive today.

Identity Theft

How long have you been held in captivity;
By the deception of the devil, our adversary?
How long will you allow your identity to be stolen?
Whose words will you believe;
The promise of the Savior or the lie of the evil one?

You have been pushed and shoved;
Don't stand on the edge precious child.
You have been defined by your past but your future is strong;
You sometimes feel helpless and hopeless and join in their song;
Thinking there is nothing good in life for you.

Come out of that dark, deserted place;
If you stay there, you will suffer and still not see God's face.
The earth is thirsty, the grass is dry;
The water is green and stagnant, it will not flow.

You might feel dejected and ashamed;
Spiritually malnourished, physically dehydrated,
And emotionally drained;
But God has not forgotten your name.

Shake the dust and wipe your feet;
You do not have to dwell in defeat;
The opportunity to move forward is at hand.

Come out of darkness and see the light;
Do not allow the devil to debase
Your character and stamp the blame.

Today is the day, in Jesus name!
Reject the devil's bondage and accept God's victory.
You prayed for release from captivity;
God has given you back your liberty.
Take it!

Mold Me

Let me be pliable Lord, mold me like clay;
Let me enter your presence daily, there's no other way.
Teach me to be gentle, teach me to be kind;
Help me to focus and not look behind.

Let me be flexible and willing to be led;
I can no longer walk alone, for fear would see me dead.
Be my potter, Lord; break, mold and reshape;
Burn all impurities without delay.

Lord, I stand ready to witness and pray;
I cannot be lackadaisical; the price is too much to pay.
I'll seek your face consistently, no more games to play;
Too many dangerous pot holes on life's crooked way.

Humble and submissive, broken now I stand;
No longer dependent on self; Lord, you are The One.
I'm ready, Dear Father, mold me to Your will;
I'm pliable, workable, yielded and still.

Self-Doubt

When feelings of insecurity arise;
Unbelief becomes possible and projects itself.
If answers are not forth coming, doubt begins to rise.

Self-doubt creeps in on quiet feet;
Making emotions unstable and frustrations upbeat.
It works against confidence and self-worth;
These must be eliminated if faith is to work.
The devil uses dark lonely streets;
He will target your location;
Run for the light and he will retreat.

Don't feed this negative unwanted force;
It will gain strength and legitimize its course;
Taking up residence within our minds;
And search for all the tainted issues it can find.

We are certainly worth much to God;
He could not bear to see our sins.
As we were aimlessly wandering
And hopelessly dying;
He sent Jesus, His Son,
To snatch us from the evil one.

We do not have to second guess God;
Some things are meant to be mysterious
Which we will never understand.
Do away with self-doubt, believe God's word;
Usher confidence in.

There Are Days

Bitter cup, tainted stew, what is life dishing you?
Feel despondent, tired and unsure?
What do you think life has in store?

Out of breath, needs unmet;
Nothing more to do but fret?
Heart racing, walls caving;
Feeling sorry for yourself?

Alone at home with your back to the wall
And no one to call?
Thinking that you should?
Not knowing if you could?
Wondering if you would?

Saying there must be a better way,
Yet doubting it will be your day;
You have contemplated long enough;
A new day dawns and it's just for you.
Make up your mind;
Time to do wonderful things
And meet beautiful people.

Stop singing your woes, we all have those;
There's good news
you can choose.
Don't give in;
You can surely win.
Where is your faith?
Let positive thinking be your trait;

Never lose heart;
God wants to be a part.
Give Him praise;
Accept the fact you're guaranteed
Much better days.

Woman with the Issue

Critics, rejecters,
Sympathizers and well-wishers;
The physical was in turmoil;
Supernatural saved the day.

Through the crowd and opposition
...she pressed...
"If I but touch."
The hem was in sight;
Strong faith made doubt redundant;
Fear was not a welcomed opponent.

Intimidation fought;
Determination won.
Hope embraced intention;
Nothing could sway her passion.

The pivotal moment was at hand;
She seized the moment and made the contact;
Faith touched power and virtue responded.

The issue removed;
Faith stood.
Hope was the woman's foretaste.
Perseverance her strength;
Healing her portion;
She was delivered.

LOVE, LIFE'S LESSONS AND APPRECIATION

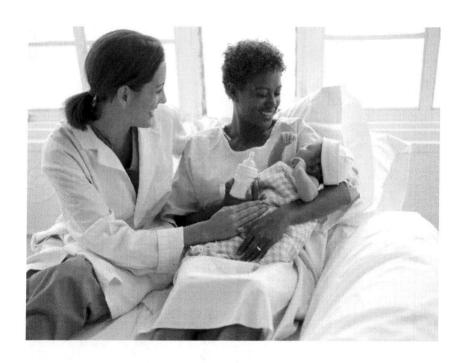

Choices

Choices embraced,
Boundaries unfenced;
Once you make them,
Right or wrong, they belong to you.

Intelligent decisions with wisdom untold;
Common sense to have and to hold;
Weigh the contents and heed the facts.

Doubt in mind?
Rule it out.
Goals in view?
Good morals won't lead you wrong.
Never refrain from good choices.
Keep loving you.

Character in tow;
Personality aglow;
God's image show.
Don't be a quitter;
Get up and go.

Showcase the heart, guard your thoughts;
Keep close the good principles taught.
No earthly gain in poor choices made;
Consequences loom, you dare not evade.
You have been charged;
Choose only the best;
God's word is sufficient to settle the rest.

Debonair Fathers

At creation, someone wonderful materialized
When God said "Let us make man."
He blew the breath of life and took creation
To its ultimate dimension.

DNA is vital and genes are dominant;
We would not be here without our Heavenly Father's input
And our earthly father's participation.

Fondly, I remember my childhood;
The fun times and the not so fun ones.
Raised eyebrows and stern glances…the warning;
A smack was not off limits if there was no heed.

Father, as a child, I saw you shed a tear or two;
Revealing your emotions and some vulnerability;
After all, you are human.
Who said that grown men do not cry?
Being too macho takes away some sensitivity.

I was there when you led family devotions;
When you spent precious hours upon your knees
Seeking God's guidance for daily decisions;
You held the family together in love and unity.

Excuse us for thinking that fathers were Supermen;
We were immature in thinking you could solve
All of life's problems.
As we grew older, we realized this was not the situation.

Thank you Heavenly Father for earthly dads,
Who uphold discipline, model integrity,
And pave positive paths for the family.
You have been chosen by God to be the foundation
On which the family structure stands.

Fathers, from our mouths and hearts to your ears and hearts;
We echo sentiments of love and appreciation.
Well done, positive fathers…Well done!

Galaxy

I choose from the galaxy tonight;
Twinkling radiant starlight bright.
Your face it knew;
Your name I lent.
Pure, ecstatic;
Incandescence flared;
Flaunted high;
Cemented in the twilight sky.
Sometimes I choose the sun;
Sometimes the moon, and give to nature
Your lovely frame.
Your beauty ensconced in crescent dew;
Crowned forever in galaxy,
Is you!

Laughter

Crackles, giggles, chuckles too;
Hilarious, wacky, loud or subdued;
A quiet smile will also do.
It will have a positive effect on you.

Laughter uninhibited, laughter free;
The true essence of laughter creates some liberty.
Without laughter we're boring and sad;
The gift of laughter makes sad moments glad.

Can't you hear it?
Can't you feel vibes that bring people to their knees?
The music of laughter ignites inner thrill;
Improves emotions if you will.
Laughter and happiness kissing sweet;
Purges thought and insecurity.

Mask-like appearances will certainly go;
Giving rise to emotions that really glow.
Once joy and humor are in sync;
Sadness disappears before you wink.

Laughter, universal language true;
Exists for all not just a few.
Transcends barriers, improves mental state;
Laughter so therapeutic and healthy.
Wouldn't you rather laugh than hate?

Sets the mood;
Changes the pace;
Prepare your face;
Laughter is contagious.
It's delicious, it's great;
Keep laughing.

Ode to Mothers

Privileged to be part of the purpose;
Ecstatic to be mothers.
The power of motherhood is not only biological
But a compelling force of bowel intuition;
And unfathomable love flowing
From the depth of all nurturing women's hearts.

Our aroma is not only perfumed but a combination of perspiration;
And the arresting freshness of baby's scent.
Love is the foundational structure of bonding enhancement.

As mothers we are always there, sampling baby foods;
Changing soiled diapers and caring for God's gifts to us.
We see the first smile, hear the first coo;
Touch the first tooth, and experience the first bite.
We kiss their tear-stained cheeks and rock them gently
To sleep at nights;
We shelter them when the so called bogeyman
Causes a fright.

We pray the first prayer, teach our children to be good citizens,
Set the boundaries, and affirm positivity.
We are there for graduation and celebrate with them
When they get their first job.

We laugh when joy is effervescent;
Offer our shoulders when tears are spent.
We calm their spirit when anger explodes;
Our hearts will forever be intertwined with theirs,
Until life ends.

We volunteer to take the hurts and pains;
Stand in front to take the blame.
Like nestling hens we watch intently,
As their vulnerabilities we rise to defend.
We see blushed faces when an admirer comes along;
And get a peek into their emotions when they experience
Their first kiss.
We stand by their side when they say
"I do" to Mr. or Miss Right.

Which mother switches off, takes a motherless vacation,
And sever that connection?
Our love and commitment connects us to our children's
Heart and soul vibrations;
Our role takes us through diverse emotions.
That's why we are called Mothers.

Olive Branch

Loyalty-laced affection that withstands hard tests;
And wins despite obstacles and fierce challenges,
Is called friendship.
It is the long arm that keeps extending an olive branch;
The consciousness that facilitates good decisions;
The mindset that allows for compromises;
With white flag resolutions.
Love in friendship enhances goals and ideals;
There's no manipulation.
When God is acknowledged in any relationship;
There is love in abundance and overflowing.
Friendship that has soul to soul connection
Is sensitive, respectful, honest and beautiful.
Keep living;
Don't stop loving;
And never forget
The value of the olive branch.

Procrastination

Time waits for no one, not for me not for you;
Be mindful of the way you spend it and the things you do.
Each moment is of value, there's no time for regrets;
Time will not linger because of fickle emotions.
When moods improve, it might be too late;
Time can be well spent or thrown away.
When opportunities come, don't hesitate;
Make them great.
Destiny must be visualized, before dreams can be realized.
Learn to love and appreciate life;
Time spent cannot be replaced.
Even at our worst moments, time is precious.
Procrastination says, wait until tomorrow,
Which has its own challenges or may never come.
But there comes a time to laugh, a time to cry;
A time to work, a time to rest;
A time to play, to sleep, to die.
Time is precious, do not procrastinate;
Use your seconds, minutes and hours wisely.
Tick tock, tick tock, tick…tock.

Somebody's Child

From way up yonder, I see him coming;
Walking, limping, disheveled, wild.
Screaming, smiling broadly;
Talking incoherently as he strides.
Exhibiting various moods and emotions;
In close proximity to my eyes.

A dirty twisted turban wrapped round
sticky matted hair;
Bare-chested chocolate colored skin;
Trying to claw its way from under dirt and grime.
His meager waistline covered with a miserly piece of cloth;
Its colors unidentifiable, tacked up with a piece of string.

A bag swings from his slender shoulder with everything he possesses.
As he draws nearer, dogs start barking, baring sharp gritted teeth;
Howling as if something sinister is imminent.
Yet on he walks, oblivious to people on the street.

I wish I knew what he was thinking.
Was he hungry or in pain?
Did he have family and wish to reunite again?
I had seen this man before on many occasions;
Sophisticated looking and classy but did not know his name.
Now here he is on the street quite helpless;
Evidently, something had gone wrong.

This unfortunate man walks around in circles;
Suddenly, he stops and walks up to me.
Should I run away like others or listen?
After all, he is somebody's child.

His unwashed body reeks.
Should I hold my breath?
Spittle settles at the corners of his mouth;
Forming a crusted sort of film.
Stale food on tobacco stained teeth quite prominent;
As he shows a crooked grin.

With hands outstretched and eyes sort of pleading;
He says, "I'm hungry, please take me in."
Why do you say, I should not have helped him?
Did you not see his frizzled state?
What if he was your kin?
I could not turn my back on one in need;
Who asked for meat; was gauntly and thin.
I gave him food; he guzzled quickly, burped loudly,
And was gone as fast as I could wink.

As he left, my eyes teared sadly; thoughts went berserk.
I could not prevent myself from asking;
What happened to him…once proud and prominent?
Frankly speaking, I thank God I'm in my right mind;
Knowing well, the divide is but razor thin.

The Old Rocking Chair

In retrospect,
I can still see the old rocking chair going
To and fro, to and fro.
On it sits an affectionate lady called Ma, who
Used to sit rocking, reading, knitting, singing.
A contagious smile on her wrinkled face;
Sometimes with a toothless grin;
At other times, with dentures bared.

For years, she sat in the same sunken spot;
Her old rocking chair going to and fro, to and fro.
Children would be huddled at her feet;
The youngest ones upon their knees.
A grand old piano played old fashioned hymns.

Once young and vibrant, now she sits knitting,
Rocking, reading, singing.
She reminisces about the good old days…
Sad ones brought misted tears to view;
But not for long… soon another smile
Would brighten up her friendly face, and
She would burst forth in yet another song…
That was Ma.

An old turtleshell eyeglass stood perched
On an already obtuse nose.
Her diminished sight an aging phenomenon;
Her hearing aid a most needed accessory.
Pictures to her were worth a million words unspoken.
Her husband long gone to rest;
Her children moved on to live their lives;
At a ripe old age of ninety, she said goodbye.
Loved ones cried, friends and well-wishers mourned her loss;
The children sang her favorite songs.
Our beloved Ma is missed, but remembered;
As her legend lives on.

Oddly, at times in my mind's eye;
I can still see the old rocking chair.
Ma's face almost obliterated with the passing of time;
Yet, the old rocking chair is still going
To and fro, to and fro.

The Power of Words

Words not verbalized are merely thoughts.
Once spoken, they cannot be retracted or erased;
They are out in the open to be scrutinized.

Let's not undermine characters when we speak;
Only use words of wisdom not words of hostility.
What kind of traits do our words portray?
Do they cause pain in any way?

Respect cannot be bought, it must be earned;
Show it and it will be returned.
It's better to use positive words to motivate;
And wonderful actions to stimulate.

If we say something without foul intent;
And someone gets hurt though not really meant;
We should be mature enough to apologize.
Once we do, we'll realize how good it feels to be forgiven;
And it does not even cost a price.
Next time before we speak let's strategize;
And make sure our words can be memorialized.

What then is Love?

Who is oblivious to the power of love?
It cannot be missed unless one has lost the zeal
For association and the fervor for passion.
Love does not exist in isolation;
It needs our emotions and soul interaction.
What then is love?
Love is the pulse and passion of the heart;
The strong force that wrestles with evil;
The peace initiator and conscience adjuster;
The hate destroyer and bond enhancer;
The joy restoring, spirit rejuvenator;
The honesty instilling, integrity coordinator;
The purifier and fulfillment adjudicator.
Love is a mind boggling, heart throbbing, hard to ignore,
Awe inspiring, God created reality.
Cherish love;
Let it bloom, blossom and flourish.
Love is a wonderful expression of God's Awesomeness.

Ripples of the Heart

Love soars to pinnacles of strong emotions
And unfurls caressing warmth that tickles the heart and soul,
When God is an integral part of the love connection.
The magnitude of love's power and the character it possesses
Allows God to get the glory.
After all, He adorns and glorifies His creation;
Love is the perfect example.
The heart of love is easy to palpate when its beats are intrinsic
And its rhythm is authentic.
Love is the force that illuminates;
The joy that effervesces;
The bond that unites, and the passion that excites.
Love is the focal point for the fruit of the spirit
to be operational.
When the seeds of love are sown and its effects are known
There must be reciprocity.
Don't just subtract from the love equation,
Be an active participant;
Give, accept and keep the love dynamic in constant motion.
Keep love's honor guarded, protected, magnified and motivated
As you celebrate the ripples of the heart.

Tribute to Aunt Polly

You exemplify a million times the phrase "Super Mom"
Words of endearment barely capture your classification;
You are the pacifying waves that keep life's sail hoisted;
The tranquil wind that keeps our emotional ship floating;
The source of sweet inspiration not only to family and friends,
But to all who come in your direction.

Aunty, you are the stabilizing force;
The fragrant balm that soothes,
When egos peak and emotions flare.
Saturated with integrity, you stand on a pedestal of love;
Which anchors and unifies the family bond

Aunty, from the bowels of your heart pours
Kindness beyond repute;
So sincere, it penetrates deeply to the core.
So tangible, it touches hearts, transforms lives and creates an
Unforgettable experience.
Blessed, so blessed, we are to be the beneficiaries of God's favor
Through you.
Thank you Aunt Polly – Mentor and "Super Mom"
From us all, we love you.

About the Author

Lorna Henningham was born in Manchester, Jamaica but grew up in the parish of Portland Jamaica, where she attended the Manchioneal Primary school and later Happy Grove High School. It was in High school that her love for English Literature began. She pursued a career in nursing and worked at the University Hospital of the West Indies for 17 years. Currently, she resides and works in South Florida. She is married to Delroy, her husband of 27 years and is the proud mother of two children and a step-daughter. She is a born again Christian and a member of the Davie Community Worship Center, where she teaches Sunday school and makes a significant contribution to ministry, through the arts.